THIS IS THE DAY
THAT THE LORD HAS MADE;
LET US

rejoice

AND BE GLAD IN IT.

Sermon Notes Journal

DATE: 1/6/19

SERMON: Purpose + Passion // Designer Jeans

Colossians 1:15-
Colossians 3:17

Howard Thurman

Chelsea Boots

Passion 2006

NOTES

The Summer Day by Mary Oliver

"Tell me, what is it you plan to do with your one wild & precious life?"

Ⓐ "To know Him & to make Him known."

Start with Why. — "For the glory of God"

Ⓑ A.W. Tozer - How can I do it to the glory of God

① What keeps you up at night & what wakes you up in the morning?

② What are you best at?

③ What are the people around you affirming in you?

TAKE AWAY· ·

This week I will focus on finding out what
brings me to life, what I do well,
& what ppl affirm me in.

The biggest enemy to purpose is uber
success in passion.

PRAYER REQUESTS· ·

Clarity & Permission

UPCOMING CHURCH EVENTS & OPPORTUNITIES· · · · · · · · · · ·

Grove Swap

DATE: 1/27/19

SERMON: Designer Jeans:

— To Desire —

Habit of   SCRIPTURE   Generosity

Succeed with your success

Romans 10:17

5-13

NOTES ·

John 3:16
The win → People hear about Jesus
Honor Him, Run, Honor your King.
G. Let your light shiiiimnneee e.
occupy That street
John 4

You don't have to be afraid.

• Write
• Podcast
• Record videos
• Build out website

Winnings: Re-Think
the Dream

"But did you plan
on succeeding?"

TAKE AWAY ·

This week I will focus on _____

_____

_____

_____

_____

_____

_____

PRAYER REQUESTS ·

_____

_____

_____

_____

_____

_____

_____

_____

_____

_____

_____

_____

_____

UPCOMING CHURCH EVENTS & OPPORTUNITIES · · · · · · · · · · ·

_____

_____

_____

_____

_____

_____

_____

DATE: 2/24

SERMON: The God you can know = Sovereignty

SCRIPTURE

All rule & All Authority.

zenith

NOTES

1 John 4:7

Agape Love is a primary motivator of God.

Agape — prefers vs. Doesn't just
tolerate. Delights in us.
Preexisting.
Not rooted in a feeling but in
the cross.
Ruler who is in love with us.

TAKE AWAY ·

This week I will focus on _____

_____

_____

_____

_____

_____

_____

PRAYER REQUESTS ·

_____

_____

_____

_____

_____

_____

_____

_____

_____

_____

_____

_____

_____

UPCOMING CHURCH EVENTS & OPPORTUNITIES · · · · · · · · · · ·

_____

_____

_____

_____

_____

_____

SCRIPTURE

NOTES

- We are more perceptive to warm hearts in a restaurant more than any other retail experience. B/c we know nourishing & love as an "inseperable experience."

Dan Cathy - CEO visit → goes in & washes hands & washes dishes.

If we don't reposition our bodies, we won't reposition our mind.

win the heart + excellence → Worship
Aggressiveness
Ambition   okay

Little Dreams Stir
NO MANS Heart

This week I will focus on

Perpetual state of inadequacy.

What is it about risk taking.

Cow calendar sold more than Sports Illustrated
~~fat~~ swim suit issue.

DATE:

SERMON: _____

┌────── SCRIPTURE ──────┐

```
┌─────────────────────────────────────────┐
│                                         │
│                                         │
│                                         │
│                                         │
│                                         │
│                                         │
│                                         │
└─────────────────────────────────────────┘
```

NOTES· ·

_____
_____
_____
_____
_____
_____
_____
_____
_____
_____
_____
_____
_____
_____
_____
_____
_____
_____
_____

TAKE AWAY ·

This week I will focus on _____

_____

_____

_____

_____

_____

_____

PRAYER REQUESTS ·

_____

_____

_____

_____

_____

_____

_____

_____

_____

_____

_____

_____

UPCOMING CHURCH EVENTS & OPPORTUNITIES · · · · · · · · · · ·

_____

_____

_____

_____

_____

_____

DATE:

SERMON: _____

SCRIPTURE

NOTES······································

TAKE AWAY ·

This week I will focus on _____

_____

_____

_____

_____

_____

_____

PRAYER REQUESTS ·

_____

_____

_____

_____

_____

_____

_____

_____

_____

_____

_____

_____

_____

UPCOMING CHURCH EVENTS & OPPORTUNITIES · · · · · · · · · · · ·

_____

_____

_____

_____

_____

_____

_____

DATE:

SERMON: _____

┌──────── SCRIPTURE ────────┐

```
┌─────────────────────────────────┐
│                                 │
│                                 │
│                                 │
│                                 │
│                                 │
│                                 │
└─────────────────────────────────┘
```

NOTES· ·

_____
_____
_____
_____
_____
_____
_____
_____
_____
_____
_____
_____
_____
_____
_____
_____
_____
_____
_____

TAKE AWAY ·

This week I will focus on _____

_____

_____

_____

_____

_____

_____

PRAYER REQUESTS ·

_____

_____

_____

_____

_____

_____

_____

_____

_____

_____

_____

_____

UPCOMING CHURCH EVENTS & OPPORTUNITIES · · · · · · · · · · ·

_____

_____

_____

_____

_____

_____

 DATE:

SERMON: _____

┌─────────── SCRIPTURE ───────────┐

┌───┐
│   │
│   │
│   │
│   │
│   │
│   │
└───┘

NOTES· ·

_____

_____

_____

_____

_____

_____

_____

_____

_____

_____

_____

_____

_____

_____

_____

_____

_____

_____

TAKE AWAY ·
This week I will focus on _____

_____
_____
_____
_____
_____
_____
_____

PRAYER REQUESTS ·

_____
_____
_____
_____
_____
_____
_____
_____
_____
_____
_____
_____
_____

UPCOMING CHURCH EVENTS & OPPORTUNITIES · · · · · · · · · · ·

_____
_____
_____
_____
_____
_____

DATE:

SERMON:_____

SCRIPTURE

NOTES··

TAKE AWAY ·······································

This week I will focus on _____

_____

_____

_____

_____

_____

_____

_____

PRAYER REQUESTS ·································

_____

_____

_____

_____

_____

_____

_____

_____

_____

_____

_____

_____

_____

_____

UPCOMING CHURCH EVENTS & OPPORTUNITIES ··········

_____

_____

_____

_____

_____

_____

_____

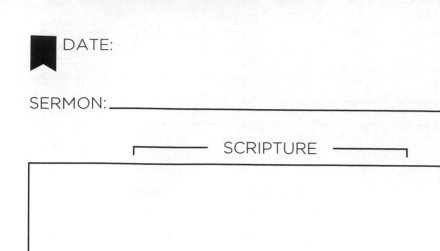

DATE:

SERMON: _____

SCRIPTURE

NOTES ·

_____
_____
_____
_____
_____
_____
_____
_____
_____
_____
_____
_____
_____
_____
_____
_____
_____
_____

TAKE AWAY ·
This week I will focus on _____

_____

_____

_____

_____

_____

_____

PRAYER REQUESTS ·

_____

_____

_____

_____

_____

_____

_____

_____

_____

_____

_____

_____

_____

_____

UPCOMING CHURCH EVENTS & OPPORTUNITIES · · · · · · · · · · ·

_____

_____

_____

_____

_____

_____

_____

_____

DATE:

SERMON: _____

──── SCRIPTURE ────

```
┌─────────────────────────────────────────┐
│                                         │
│                                         │
│                                         │
│                                         │
│                                         │
│                                         │
│                                         │
└─────────────────────────────────────────┘
```

NOTES ·

_____
_____
_____
_____
_____
_____
_____
_____
_____
_____
_____
_____
_____
_____
_____
_____
_____
_____
_____

TAKE AWAY ··

This week I will focus on _____

_____

_____

_____

_____

_____

_____

PRAYER REQUESTS ···································

_____

_____

_____

_____

_____

_____

_____

_____

_____

_____

_____

_____

UPCOMING CHURCH EVENTS & OPPORTUNITIES ··········

_____

_____

_____

_____

_____

_____

_____

DATE:

SERMON: _____

SCRIPTURE

NOTES· ·

_____

_____

_____

_____

_____

_____

_____

_____

_____

_____

_____

_____

_____

_____

_____

_____

_____

_____

TAKE AWAY ·
This week I will focus on _____

_____

_____

_____

_____

_____

_____

_____

PRAYER REQUESTS· ·

_____

_____

_____

_____

_____

_____

_____

_____

_____

_____

_____

_____

_____

_____

UPCOMING CHURCH EVENTS & OPPORTUNITIES· · · · · · · · · · ·

_____

_____

_____

_____

_____

_____

_____

_____

DATE:

SERMON: _____

SCRIPTURE

NOTES ·

_____

_____

_____

_____

_____

_____

_____

_____

_____

_____

_____

_____

_____

_____

_____

_____

_____

_____

_____

_____

TAKE AWAY··

This week I will focus on _____

_____

_____

_____

_____

_____

_____

_____

PRAYER REQUESTS·····································

_____

_____

_____

_____

_____

_____

_____

_____

_____

_____

_____

_____

_____

_____

UPCOMING CHURCH EVENTS & OPPORTUNITIES···········

_____

_____

_____

_____

_____

_____

_____

_____

DATE:

SERMON:_____

SCRIPTURE

NOTES···

TAKE AWAY ·

This week I will focus on _____

_____

_____

_____

_____

_____

_____

PRAYER REQUESTS ·

_____

_____

_____

_____

_____

_____

_____

_____

_____

_____

_____

_____

_____

UPCOMING CHURCH EVENTS & OPPORTUNITIES · · · · · · · · · · ·

_____

_____

_____

_____

_____

_____

_____

DATE:

SERMON:_____

SCRIPTURE

NOTES···

TAKE AWAY ·

This week I will focus on _____

_____

_____

_____

_____

_____

_____

_____

PRAYER REQUESTS ·

_____

_____

_____

_____

_____

_____

_____

_____

_____

_____

_____

_____

_____

_____

UPCOMING CHURCH EVENTS & OPPORTUNITIES · · · · · · · · · · ·

_____

_____

_____

_____

_____

_____

_____

DATE:

SERMON: _____

┌─────── SCRIPTURE ───────┐

NOTES· ·

TAKE AWAY· ·

This week I will focus on _____

_____

_____

_____

_____

_____

_____

_____

PRAYER REQUESTS· ·

_____

_____

_____

_____

_____

_____

_____

_____

_____

_____

_____

_____

_____

_____

_____

_____

UPCOMING CHURCH EVENTS & OPPORTUNITIES· · · · · · · · · · ·

_____

_____

_____

_____

_____

_____

_____

_____

DATE:

SERMON: _____

┌─────── SCRIPTURE ───────┐

┌───┐
│   │
│   │
│   │
│   │
│   │
│   │
│   │
│   │
└───┘

NOTES ·

_____

_____

_____

_____

_____

_____

_____

_____

_____

_____

_____

_____

_____

_____

_____

_____

_____

_____

_____

TAKE AWAY ·
This week I will focus on _____

_____
_____
_____
_____
_____
_____

PRAYER REQUESTS ·

_____
_____
_____
_____
_____
_____
_____
_____
_____
_____
_____
_____
_____

UPCOMING CHURCH EVENTS & OPPORTUNITIES · · · · · · · · · · ·

_____
_____
_____
_____
_____
_____
_____

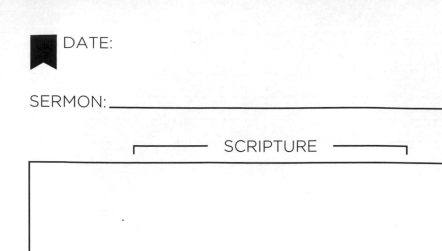

DATE:

SERMON: _____

┌──────── SCRIPTURE ────────┐

NOTES ·

_____
_____
_____
_____
_____
_____
_____
_____
_____
_____
_____
_____
_____
_____
_____
_____
_____
_____
_____

TAKE AWAY ·

This week I will focus on _____

_____

_____

_____

_____

_____

_____

_____

PRAYER REQUESTS ·

_____

_____

_____

_____

_____

_____

_____

_____

_____

_____

_____

_____

_____

_____

UPCOMING CHURCH EVENTS & OPPORTUNITIES · · · · · · · · · · ·

_____

_____

_____

_____

_____

_____

_____

_____

DATE:

SERMON: _____

┌─────── SCRIPTURE ───────┐

┌───┐
│   │
│   │
│   │
│   │
│   │
│   │
│   │
└───┘

NOTES· ·

_____

_____

_____

_____

_____

_____

_____

_____

_____

_____

_____

_____

_____

_____

_____

_____

_____

_____

_____

TAKE AWAY ·

This week I will focus on _____

_____

_____

_____

_____

_____

_____

_____

PRAYER REQUESTS ·

_____

_____

_____

_____

_____

_____

_____

_____

_____

_____

_____

_____

_____

UPCOMING CHURCH EVENTS & OPPORTUNITIES · · · · · · · · · · ·

_____

_____

_____

_____

_____

_____

_____

DATE:

SERMON: _____

―――――――――― SCRIPTURE ――――――――――

NOTES··

TAKE AWAY ·

This week I will focus on _____

_____

_____

_____

_____

_____

_____

PRAYER REQUESTS ·

_____

_____

_____

_____

_____

_____

_____

_____

_____

_____

_____

_____

UPCOMING CHURCH EVENTS & OPPORTUNITIES · · · · · · · · · · ·

_____

_____

_____

_____

_____

_____

_____

DATE:

SERMON:_____

┌─────── SCRIPTURE ───────┐

NOTES· ·

TAKE AWAY ·
This week I will focus on _____

_____

_____

_____

_____

_____

_____

PRAYER REQUESTS ·

_____

_____

_____

_____

_____

_____

_____

_____

_____

_____

_____

_____

UPCOMING CHURCH EVENTS & OPPORTUNITIES · · · · · · · · · · ·

_____

_____

_____

_____

_____

_____

_____

DATE:

SERMON: _____

SCRIPTURE

NOTES ·

TAKE AWAY·······································

This week I will focus on _____

_____

_____

_____

_____

_____

_____

PRAYER REQUESTS·································

_____

_____

_____

_____

_____

_____

_____

_____

_____

_____

_____

_____

UPCOMING CHURCH EVENTS & OPPORTUNITIES··········

_____

_____

_____

_____

_____

_____

_____

DATE:

SERMON: _____

SCRIPTURE

NOTES· ·

TAKE AWAY· ·

This week I will focus on _____

_____

_____

_____

_____

_____

_____

PRAYER REQUESTS· ·

_____

_____

_____

_____

_____

_____

_____

_____

_____

_____

_____

_____

UPCOMING CHURCH EVENTS & OPPORTUNITIES· · · · · · · · · · ·

_____

_____

_____

_____

_____

_____

_____

DATE:

SERMON: _____

SCRIPTURE

NOTES ·

_____
_____
_____
_____
_____
_____
_____
_____
_____
_____
_____
_____
_____
_____
_____
_____
_____
_____
_____

TAKE AWAY ·

This week I will focus on _____

_____

_____

_____

_____

_____

_____

_____

PRAYER REQUESTS ·

_____

_____

_____

_____

_____

_____

_____

_____

_____

_____

_____

_____

_____

_____

_____

UPCOMING CHURCH EVENTS & OPPORTUNITIES · · · · · · · · · · ·

_____

_____

_____

_____

_____

_____

_____

_____

DATE:

SERMON: _____

┌─────── SCRIPTURE ───────┐

┌───┐
│   │
│   │
│   │
│   │
│   │
│   │
│   │
│   │
└───┘

NOTES··
_____
_____
_____
_____
_____
_____
_____
_____
_____
_____
_____
_____
_____
_____
_____
_____
_____
_____
_____
_____

TAKE AWAY ·

This week I will focus on _____

_____

_____

_____

_____

_____

_____

_____

PRAYER REQUESTS ·

_____

_____

_____

_____

_____

_____

_____

_____

_____

_____

_____

_____

_____

_____

_____

UPCOMING CHURCH EVENTS & OPPORTUNITIES · · · · · · · · · · ·

_____

_____

_____

_____

_____

_____

_____

_____

DATE:

SERMON: _____

┌────── SCRIPTURE ──────┐

┌─────────────────────────────────────┐
│   │
│   │
│   │
│   │
│   │
│   │
│   │
└─────────────────────────────────────┘

NOTES· ·

_____
_____
_____
_____
_____
_____
_____
_____
_____
_____
_____
_____
_____
_____
_____
_____
_____
_____
_____

TAKE AWAY ·

This week I will focus on _____

_____

_____

_____

_____

_____

_____

PRAYER REQUESTS ·

_____

_____

_____

_____

_____

_____

_____

_____

_____

_____

_____

_____

_____

UPCOMING CHURCH EVENTS & OPPORTUNITIES · · · · · · · · · · · ·

_____

_____

_____

_____

_____

_____

_____

DATE:

SERMON: _____

┌──────── SCRIPTURE ────────┐

NOTES· ·

TAKE AWAY· ·

This week I will focus on _____

_____

_____

_____

_____

_____

_____

PRAYER REQUESTS· ·

_____

_____

_____

_____

_____

_____

_____

_____

_____

_____

_____

_____

UPCOMING CHURCH EVENTS & OPPORTUNITIES· · · · · · · · · · ·

_____

_____

_____

_____

_____

_____

_____

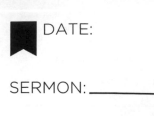
DATE:

SERMON: _____

────── SCRIPTURE ──────

NOTES ·

TAKE AWAY ·

This week I will focus on _____

_____

_____

_____

_____

_____

_____

PRAYER REQUESTS ·

_____

_____

_____

_____

_____

_____

_____

_____

_____

_____

_____

_____

_____

UPCOMING CHURCH EVENTS & OPPORTUNITIES · · · · · · · · · · ·

_____

_____

_____

_____

_____

_____

_____

DATE:

SERMON: _____

NOTES· ·

_____
_____
_____
_____
_____
_____
_____
_____
_____
_____
_____
_____
_____
_____
_____
_____
_____
_____
_____

TAKE AWAY ·

This week I will focus on _____

_____

_____

_____

_____

_____

_____

PRAYER REQUESTS ·

_____

_____

_____

_____

_____

_____

_____

_____

_____

_____

_____

_____

UPCOMING CHURCH EVENTS & OPPORTUNITIES · · · · · · · · · · ·

_____

_____

_____

_____

_____

_____

_____

DATE:

SERMON: _____

SCRIPTURE

NOTES ·

_____

_____

_____

_____

_____

_____

_____

_____

_____

_____

_____

_____

_____

_____

_____

_____

_____

_____

TAKE AWAY ·

This week I will focus on _____

_____

_____

_____

_____

_____

_____

_____

PRAYER REQUESTS· ·

_____

_____

_____

_____

_____

_____

_____

_____

_____

_____

_____

_____

_____

UPCOMING CHURCH EVENTS & OPPORTUNITIES· · · · · · · · · · ·

_____

_____

_____

_____

_____

_____

_____

_____

DATE:

SERMON: _____

┌───── SCRIPTURE ─────┐

┌─────────────────────────────────────┐
│   │
│   │
│   │
│   │
│   │
│   │
│   │
└─────────────────────────────────────┘

NOTES· ·

_____
_____
_____
_____
_____
_____
_____
_____
_____
_____
_____
_____
_____
_____
_____
_____
_____
_____
_____
_____
_____

TAKE AWAY ·

This week I will focus on _____

_____

_____

_____

_____

_____

_____

PRAYER REQUESTS ·

_____

_____

_____

_____

_____

_____

_____

_____

_____

_____

_____

_____

UPCOMING CHURCH EVENTS & OPPORTUNITIES · · · · · · · · · · ·

_____

_____

_____

_____

_____

_____

_____

DATE:

SERMON: _____

SCRIPTURE

NOTES· ·

_____
_____
_____
_____
_____
_____
_____
_____
_____
_____
_____
_____
_____
_____
_____
_____
_____
_____
_____

TAKE AWAY ·

This week I will focus on _____

_____

_____

_____

_____

_____

_____

PRAYER REQUESTS ·

_____

_____

_____

_____

_____

_____

_____

_____

_____

_____

_____

_____

UPCOMING CHURCH EVENTS & OPPORTUNITIES · · · · · · · · · · · ·

_____

_____

_____

_____

_____

_____

_____

DATE:

SERMON:_____

SCRIPTURE

NOTES··

_____
_____
_____
_____
_____
_____
_____
_____
_____
_____
_____
_____
_____
_____
_____
_____
_____
_____
_____
_____
_____

TAKE AWAY ·
This week I will focus on _____

_____

_____

_____

_____

_____

_____

_____

PRAYER REQUESTS ·

_____

_____

_____

_____

_____

_____

_____

_____

_____

_____

_____

_____

_____

UPCOMING CHURCH EVENTS & OPPORTUNITIES · · · · · · · · · · · ·

_____

_____

_____

_____

_____

_____

_____

_____

DATE:

SERMON:_____

SCRIPTURE
┌─────────────────────────────────┐
│   │
│   │
│   │
│   │
│   │
│   │
└─────────────────────────────────┘

NOTES· ·

_____
_____
_____
_____
_____
_____
_____
_____
_____
_____
_____
_____
_____
_____
_____
_____
_____
_____

TAKE AWAY ·
This week I will focus on _____

_____
_____
_____
_____
_____
_____
_____

PRAYER REQUESTS ·

_____
_____
_____
_____
_____
_____
_____
_____
_____
_____
_____
_____
_____

UPCOMING CHURCH EVENTS & OPPORTUNITIES · · · · · · · · · · ·

_____
_____
_____
_____
_____
_____
_____

DATE:

SERMON: _____

SCRIPTURE

NOTES···

TAKE AWAY ·
This week I will focus on _____

_____

_____

_____

_____

_____

_____

_____

PRAYER REQUESTS ·

_____

_____

_____

_____

_____

_____

_____

_____

_____

_____

_____

_____

_____

_____

UPCOMING CHURCH EVENTS & OPPORTUNITIES · · · · · · · · · · · ·

_____

_____

_____

_____

_____

_____

_____

DATE:

SERMON:_____

SCRIPTURE

NOTES· ·

_____
_____
_____
_____
_____
_____
_____
_____
_____
_____
_____
_____
_____
_____
_____
_____
_____
_____
_____
_____

TAKE AWAY ·
This week I will focus on _____

_____

_____

_____

_____

_____

_____

PRAYER REQUESTS ·

_____

_____

_____

_____

_____

_____

_____

_____

_____

_____

_____

_____

_____

_____

UPCOMING CHURCH EVENTS & OPPORTUNITIES · · · · · · · · · · ·

_____

_____

_____

_____

_____

_____

_____

DATE:

SERMON: _____

┌────────── SCRIPTURE ──────────┐

NOTES···

TAKE AWAY ·

This week I will focus on _____

_____

_____

_____

_____

_____

_____

PRAYER REQUESTS ·

_____

_____

_____

_____

_____

_____

_____

_____

_____

_____

_____

_____

_____

UPCOMING CHURCH EVENTS & OPPORTUNITIES · · · · · · · · · · ·

_____

_____

_____

_____

_____

_____

_____

DATE:

SERMON:

SCRIPTURE

NOTES

TAKE AWAY ·

This week I will focus on _____

_____

_____

_____

_____

_____

_____

_____

PRAYER REQUESTS ·

_____

_____

_____

_____

_____

_____

_____

_____

_____

_____

_____

_____

_____

UPCOMING CHURCH EVENTS & OPPORTUNITIES · · · · · · · · · · ·

_____

_____

_____

_____

_____

_____

_____

_____

DATE:

SERMON: _____

┌─────── SCRIPTURE ───────┐

┌──┐
│   │
│   │
│   │
│   │
│   │
│   │
│   │
│   │
│   │
└──┘

NOTES ·

_____

_____

_____

_____

_____

_____

_____

_____

_____

_____

_____

_____

_____

_____

_____

_____

_____

_____

TAKE AWAY ·

This week I will focus on _____

_____

_____

_____

_____

_____

_____

_____

PRAYER REQUESTS ·

_____

_____

_____

_____

_____

_____

_____

_____

_____

_____

_____

_____

_____

UPCOMING CHURCH EVENTS & OPPORTUNITIES · · · · · · · · · · · ·

_____

_____

_____

_____

_____

_____

_____

DATE:

SERMON: _____

┌─── SCRIPTURE ───┐

┌─────────────────────────────────────┐
│   │
│   │
│   │
│   │
│   │
│   │
│   │
└─────────────────────────────────────┘

NOTES···

_____
_____
_____
_____
_____
_____
_____
_____
_____
_____
_____
_____
_____
_____
_____
_____
_____
_____
_____

TAKE AWAY ·

This week I will focus on _____

_____

_____

_____

_____

_____

_____

PRAYER REQUESTS ·

_____

_____

_____

_____

_____

_____

_____

_____

_____

_____

_____

_____

UPCOMING CHURCH EVENTS & OPPORTUNITIES · · · · · · · · · · ·

_____

_____

_____

_____

_____

_____

_____

DATE:

SERMON: _____

┌────── SCRIPTURE ──────┐

┌───┐
│   │
│   │
│   │
│   │
│   │
│   │
│   │
└───┘

NOTES· ·

_____
_____
_____
_____
_____
_____
_____
_____
_____
_____
_____
_____
_____
_____
_____
_____
_____
_____
_____

TAKE AWAY ·

This week I will focus on _____

_____

_____

_____

_____

_____

_____

PRAYER REQUESTS ·

_____

_____

_____

_____

_____

_____

_____

_____

_____

_____

UPCOMING CHURCH EVENTS & OPPORTUNITIES · · · · · · · · · · · ·

_____

_____

_____

_____

_____

_____

DATE:

SERMON: _____

┌──────── SCRIPTURE ────────┐

```
┌─────────────────────────────────────────┐
│                                         │
│                                         │
│                                         │
│                                         │
│                                         │
│                                         │
│                                         │
└─────────────────────────────────────────┘
```

NOTES··

_____
_____
_____
_____
_____
_____
_____
_____
_____
_____
_____
_____
_____
_____
_____
_____
_____
_____
_____
_____

TAKE AWAY ·

This week I will focus on _____

_____

_____

_____

_____

_____

_____

_____

PRAYER REQUESTS ·

_____

_____

_____

_____

_____

_____

_____

_____

_____

_____

_____

_____

_____

_____

UPCOMING CHURCH EVENTS & OPPORTUNITIES · · · · · · · · · · ·

_____

_____

_____

_____

_____

_____

_____

DATE:

SERMON:_____

SCRIPTURE

NOTES ·

TAKE AWAY ·
This week I will focus on _____

_____

_____

_____

_____

_____

_____

PRAYER REQUESTS ·

_____

_____

_____

_____

_____

_____

_____

_____

_____

_____

_____

_____

_____

UPCOMING CHURCH EVENTS & OPPORTUNITIES · · · · · · · · · · ·

_____

_____

_____

_____

_____

_____

DATE:

SERMON:_____

┌─────── SCRIPTURE ───────┐

┌───┐
│   │
│   │
│   │
│   │
│   │
│   │
└───┘

NOTES· ·

_____
_____
_____
_____
_____
_____
_____
_____
_____
_____
_____
_____
_____
_____
_____
_____
_____
_____
_____

TAKE AWAY ·

This week I will focus on _____

_____

_____

_____

_____

_____

_____

_____

PRAYER REQUESTS ·

_____

_____

_____

_____

_____

_____

_____

_____

_____

_____

_____

_____

_____

UPCOMING CHURCH EVENTS & OPPORTUNITIES · · · · · · · · · · ·

_____

_____

_____

_____

_____

_____

_____

DATE:

SERMON:_____

┌─────── SCRIPTURE ───────┐

┌───┐
│   │
│   │
│   │
│   │
│   │
│   │
│   │
└───┘

NOTES· ·

_____

_____

_____

_____

_____

_____

_____

_____

_____

_____

_____

_____

_____

_____

_____

_____

_____

_____

TAKE AWAY ·

This week I will focus on _____

_____

_____

_____

_____

_____

_____

PRAYER REQUESTS ·

_____

_____

_____

_____

_____

_____

_____

_____

_____

_____

_____

_____

_____

UPCOMING CHURCH EVENTS & OPPORTUNITIES · · · · · · · · · · ·

_____

_____

_____

_____

_____

_____

_____

DATE:

SERMON: _____

───── SCRIPTURE ─────

NOTES ···

TAKE AWAY··

This week I will focus on _____

_____

_____

_____

_____

_____

_____

_____

PRAYER REQUESTS···

_____

_____

_____

_____

_____

_____

_____

_____

_____

_____

_____

_____

_____

UPCOMING CHURCH EVENTS & OPPORTUNITIES··············

_____

_____

_____

_____

_____

_____

_____

DATE:

SERMON: _____

┌──────── SCRIPTURE ────────┐

┌─────────────────────────────────────┐
│   │
│   │
│   │
│   │
│   │
│   │
│   │
└─────────────────────────────────────┘

NOTES···

TAKE AWAY ·
This week I will focus on _____

_____

_____

_____

_____

_____

_____

PRAYER REQUESTS ·

_____

_____

_____

_____

_____

_____

_____

_____

_____

_____

_____

_____

UPCOMING CHURCH EVENTS & OPPORTUNITIES · · · · · · · · · · ·

_____

_____

_____

_____

_____

_____

_____

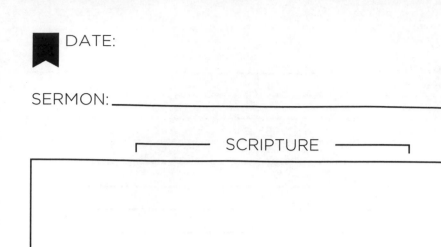

DATE:

SERMON: _____

SCRIPTURE

NOTES ·

TAKE AWAY ·

This week I will focus on _____

_____

_____

_____

_____

_____

_____

PRAYER REQUESTS ·

_____

_____

_____

_____

_____

_____

_____

_____

_____

_____

_____

_____

UPCOMING CHURCH EVENTS & OPPORTUNITIES · · · · · · · · · · ·

_____

_____

_____

_____

_____

_____

_____

DATE:

SERMON: _____

SCRIPTURE

NOTES· ·

_____
_____
_____
_____
_____
_____
_____
_____
_____
_____
_____
_____
_____
_____
_____
_____
_____
_____
_____
_____
_____

TAKE AWAY ·
This week I will focus on _____

_____
_____
_____
_____
_____
_____
_____

PRAYER REQUESTS ·

_____
_____
_____
_____
_____
_____
_____
_____
_____
_____
_____
_____
_____

UPCOMING CHURCH EVENTS & OPPORTUNITIES · · · · · · · · · · · ·

_____
_____
_____
_____
_____
_____
_____

DATE:

SERMON: _____

┌───── SCRIPTURE ─────┐

┌─────────────────────────────────────┐
│   │
│   │
│   │
│   │
│   │
│   │
│   │
└─────────────────────────────────────┘

NOTES···

_____
_____
_____
_____
_____
_____
_____
_____
_____
_____
_____
_____
_____
_____
_____
_____
_____
_____
_____

TAKE AWAY ·

This week I will focus on _____

_____

_____

_____

_____

_____

_____

_____

PRAYER REQUESTS ·

_____

_____

_____

_____

_____

_____

_____

_____

_____

_____

_____

_____

_____

_____

UPCOMING CHURCH EVENTS & OPPORTUNITIES · · · · · · · · · · ·

_____

_____

_____

_____

_____

_____

_____

_____

DATE:

SERMON: _____

SCRIPTURE

NOTES· ·

_____
_____
_____
_____
_____
_____
_____
_____
_____
_____
_____
_____
_____
_____
_____
_____
_____
_____
_____
_____

TAKE AWAY ·
This week I will focus on _____

_____
_____
_____
_____
_____
_____
_____

PRAYER REQUESTS ·

_____
_____
_____
_____
_____
_____
_____
_____
_____
_____
_____
_____
_____
_____

UPCOMING CHURCH EVENTS & OPPORTUNITIES · · · · · · · · · · ·

_____
_____
_____
_____
_____
_____
_____
_____

DATE:

SERMON: _____

┌──────── SCRIPTURE ────────┐
┌───┐
│   │
│   │
│   │
│   │
│   │
│   │
│   │
│   │
└───┘

NOTES· ·

_____

_____

_____

_____

_____

_____

_____

_____

_____

_____

_____

_____

_____

_____

_____

_____

_____

_____

_____

TAKE AWAY· ·
This week I will focus on _____

_____

_____

_____

_____

_____

_____

PRAYER REQUESTS· ·

_____

_____

_____

_____

_____

_____

_____

_____

_____

_____

_____

_____

_____

UPCOMING CHURCH EVENTS & OPPORTUNITIES· · · · · · · · · · ·

_____

_____

_____

_____

_____

_____

_____

DATE:

SERMON: _____

┌──────── SCRIPTURE ────────┐

┌──┐
│   │
│   │
│   │
│   │
│   │
│   │
│   │
│   │
└──┘

NOTES· ·

_____

_____

_____

_____

_____

_____

_____

_____

_____

_____

_____

_____

_____

_____

_____

_____

_____

_____

_____

TAKE AWAY ·································

This week I will focus on _____

_____

_____

_____

_____

_____

_____

PRAYER REQUESTS ·······························

_____

_____

_____

_____

_____

_____

_____

_____

_____

_____

_____

_____

_____

UPCOMING CHURCH EVENTS & OPPORTUNITIES ··········

_____

_____

_____

_____

_____

_____